Paralegal Notes

This book is intended as a reference and not to be used as legal advice.

Copyright 2012

Table of Contents

Introduction to Research

National Association of Legal Assistants (Largest).

National Federation of Paralegal Associations (2nd Largest). Student membership $45.00 a year.

Paralegals can represent clients before some administrative agencies (IRS Form 23 & 2587). Mediation tries to get both sides to work it out. Arbitration makes decisions. Paralegals can be mediators - no law license needed.

Legal Document Assistants are certified; work in the courthouse etc...

Primary Sources of Law:

    1. Constitutions

    2. Statutes

    3. Administrative Rules and Regulations

    4. Case law

Mandatory Law:

    1. Primary source of law

    2. From the same jurisdiction

    3. From a higher court. The U.S. Constitution, Federal Statutes and U.S. Supreme Court decisions are mandatory for everyone.

Persuasive Law: Secondary sources of law, Primary law from another jurisdiction, Primary law from a lower court.

All sources of law fall under one of three categories: Primary mandatory law, Primary persuasive law, secondary persuasive law.

General order for primary sources of law:

    1. U.S. Constitution

    2. Federal Statutes

    3. Federal Administrative Code

    4. U.S. Supreme Court decisions

    5. State Constitution

    6. State Statutes

    7. State Administrative Code

    8. State Supreme Court decisions

Examples:

1. A Wisconsin statute: Primary Mandatory
2. A Wisconsin supreme court case: Primary Mandatory
3. A Wisconsin Court of Appeals case: Primary Mandatory
4. A section of the Illinois Administrative Code: Primary Persuasive
5. A 7th Circuit Court of Appeals case: Secondary Persuasive
6. A section of the Uniform Commercial Code: Secondary Persuasive

Bankruptcy 2005 = Creditors have edge

Voluntary and Involuntary Bankruptcy

Chapter 7 = Liquidation, person, partnerships and corporations. No insurance or banks.

Chapter 11 = Reorganize

Chapter 13 = Individuals, repayments

Title 11 USC

WI exemptions on Bankruptcy: $75K on house.

Reaffirmation is a new agreement with lender.

Landlord can't evict for discharged debt.

Equitable Remedies:

1. Specific Performance – order to perform what was promised; - it is unique and used when money is not adequate.
2. Injunction – order for defendant to do or refrain from doing an act.
3. Rescission, Restitution, Declaratory Relief, Quiet Title, and Provisional Relief.

Torts: Cannot sue for dollars. Prayer for relief.

Three types of torts:

1. Intentional
2. Unintentional/Negligence
3. Strict Liability

Elements of Negligence:

1. Legal Duty: Breach of the legal duty
2. Causation proximate cause: Direct result or reasonably probable consequence.

3. Injury or damages Negligence: Duty of Care.

4. "Reasonable person" standard: how that person should act, what risks that person should expect to arise from conduct. Each person responsible for own behavior.

Injury and Damages must be legally recognizable and actual Damages allowed.

Compensatory damages to reimburse or "make whole" punitive or exemplary damages to punish and deter future similar conduct.

Comparative negligence: 50% plaintiff's fault and there is no recovery. Percentage of recovery is tied to what percentage of fault you are at.

Proximate cause: based on fore-seeing ability, indirect, but predictable effect.

Strict Liability: Dangerous animals, defective products, failure to warn.

Tort Cases:

1. Assault Intentional: Unexcused act . . . creates in another person a reasonable apprehension or fear . . . of immediate harmful or offensive contact.

2. Battery Intentional: Unexcused act . . . harmful or offensive physical contact. Can include something attached to the body.

3. Conversion (theft): Wrongful taking of personal property from its rightful owner or possessor placed in the service of another. Deprives the rightful owner of the use of the property. Civil side of criminal act of theft.

4. Slander: Wrongfully hurting a person's good reputation (false oral statement). Must be communicated to someone other than the defamed party.

5. Libel: Wrongfully hurting a person's good reputation by false written statement. Must show actual malice and be communicated to someone other than the defamed party. Includes the internet. Intentional infliction of emotional distress;-intentional act offensive to a reasonable person creates emotional distress that is harmful to the plaintiff.

6. False Imprisonment: Intentional confinement or restraint of another person without justification. Physical Barriers, physical restraint, and threats of physical force.

7. Trespass to Land: A person enters without permission onto, above, or below the surface of land that is owned by another or causes anything to enter onto the land or remains on the land or permits anything to remain on it. Actual harm is not required.

8. Wrongful interference: There is a legal contract. Defendant knew of the contract. Defendant improperly induced 3rd party to breach or made performance impossible. Injury to plaintiff.

9. Invasion of Privacy: Intrusion in an individual's affairs or seclusion (reasonable expectation of privacy). Publication of information that places a person in a false light. Public disclosure of private facts (objectionable to reasonable person).

10. Misrepresentation Misstatement or omission of a material fact made with the intent of deceiving another. An untrue statement of fact.

Contracts:
1. Mutual agreement (offer + acceptance)
2. Consideration – both sides
3. Contractual Capacity
4. Legality 18 years old

Defenses to enforceability:

No mutual agreement, mutual mistake, fraud, undue influence, duress, unconscionable contract (shockingly unfair).

Contracts that must be in writing to be enforceable:
1. Marriage
2. Year (by its terms, will last longer than 1 year)
3. Land
4. Executors (wills, trusts)
5. Goods over $500
6. Sureties (agree to pay someone else's debt)

Sales Contracts are covered by the Uniform Commercial Code (UCC). The UCC was created in 1952 and incorporated into statutes by most states. The Code provides a national approach to the interpretation of contracts for the sale of goods across the 50 states.

Liability for Contracts:

Principal solely liable for agent's acts performed within actual authority granted when principal is fully disclosed third party knows there of an agency relationship and the identity of the principal. Both principal and agent are liable for agent's acts performed within actual authority granted when principal is partially disclosed. Agent solely liable for agent's acts performed within actual authority granted when principal is undisclosed Third party does not know: there is an agency relationship and the identity of the principal Agent can obtain indemnification from principal. Principal also solely liable for agent's acts performed within apparent authority. Principal can obtain indemnification from agent for unauthorized acts.

Tort Liability:

Agents are liable for their own torts. Principal liable for agent's negligent acts committed in the course and scope of the agency.

Warranties:

1. Express Warranties: Actual representations of the nature of goods being sold. Representation must be part of the reason the buyer made the purchase.
2. Implied warranty of merchantability: Applies to merchants only, goods are reasonably fit for their general purpose.
3. Implied warranty of fitness for particular purpose: Merchant or non-merchant seller, knows buyer's particular purpose. Knows buyer relies on seller's expertise and selects suitable goods for the buyer.

Case numbers:

2005-FA-743 = Year 2005 Family Court 743rd case.

When this case is appealed it will get an appellate docket number. Appellate number 2006-AP-60 = Year 2006 Appeals 60th case appealed that year. When the case is decided it will get a publication date (Public Domain). The same goes for the Supreme Court. It will get a filing date and a publication or ruling date. See chapter titled Court Case Abbreviations for letter identification of cases.

C.J. = Chief Judge or Justice. Justice is from the Supreme Court and judges are in the rest of the courts.

J.: Justice or Judge.

J.J.: Justices or Judges.

P.J.: Presiding Judge.

Pie = π = Plaintiff v. Delta = $\triangle$ = Defendant

Federal Court Jurisdiction: Diversity and over $75K

Personal Jurisdiction: Authority or power over the parties.

Need subject matter and personal jurisdiction for a suit. Individuals can contract for jurisdiction. States created long arm statutes to have jurisdiction over sellers in a state.

In Rem Jurisdiction: Property has to be within jurisdiction of a state (subject of lawsuit).

Subject Matter Jurisdiction: Authority that a court has to hear a case (bankruptcy, family court, etc...).

Quasi In Rem Jurisdiction: Even if property is not subject of lawsuit the court achieves jurisdiction over the defendant by owning property in the state.

Venue: Where the case is heard. It is the defendants' job to challenge the venue.

Wis. Stat. § 100.20 (5) (2011) Any person suffering pecuniary loss because of a violation by any other person of any order issued under this section may sue for damages therefore in any court of competent jurisdiction and shall recover twice the amount of such pecuniary loss, together with costs, including a reasonable attorney's fee.

Model Penal Code: Developed by the American Law Institute to assist legislatures to update and standardize criminal law. Wisconsin has not adopted the Model Penal Code.

Prosecutors are bound by the Model Code of Professional Responsibility and the Model Rules of Professional Conduct.

Researching the Law in Wisconsin

West Law and Lexis are popular online research tools and require a subscription. Loislaw and VersusLaw are smaller, less expensive online tools, and WI Fast Case is free for licensed attorneys.

Find a topic or subject by initiating a search with a thesaurus, Black's Law Dictionary or index to WI Statutes to find descriptive words or phrases to begin a research project. Legal encyclopedias can be used to look up a subject. Three predominant legal encyclopedias exist: 1. Corpus Juris Secundum 2. West's Legal Encyclopedias 3. American Jurisprudence.

Free Online Tools

1. Wilawlibrary.gov: Go to "legal topics", "**start search**" to find a list of available **subjects to research**. Many resources available on this website including federal and state forms.

2. Wisbar.org: Go to "**Lawyer Search**" to find the history and status of any Wisconsin licensed attorney. Also available at that website is a lawyer referral and information service.

3. Govtrack.us is good for searching bills, resolutions, and members of congress.

4. Wcca.wicourts.gov (WI Circuit Court Access): Under "search" find a **case** by name or case number. Select a case & click on "Court record events" to find all filings in that case.

5. Wicourts.gov: Many Wisconsin court **forms** available and **court rules**.

    A. Under "Services" select "For the Public" and below them is a self-help law center and links for complaints against attorneys and judges.

    B. Under "Opinions" select "Appeals or Supreme Court" to search case law by citation (inoperative search at time of writing). Public Domain Citation # will bring up a PDF case file. Use the keyword search function which will further enable you to use advance search for limited **words and phrases**. A citation in the keyword search will pull up a PDF case file.

6. Wscca.wicourt.gov (Wisconsin Supreme Court & Court of Appeals): Case search by case number, party, public domain citation, and official publishers which can reveal parallel citations.

7. Legis.wisconsin.gov: Go to "Wisconsin Law" and select **acts, codes** (with index) and **statutes** (with index). Also using Google and simply typing "WI Stat" followed by subject being investigated will generally lead to prevailing statutes in that subject matter. Wikipedia is starting to show promise of good definitions with case law cited and explained.

8. NCSC.org is the National Center for State Courts if information is needed for other state courts.

9. WDFI.org/apps/CorpSearch/Search.aspx?: To serve a complaint on a corporation, go to Wisconsin Department of Financial Institutions WDFI and search "corporations" and search "corporate records". The person to serve will be listed for that company.

10. Utilize Wisconsin Pleading and Practice for guidance through every stage of a case or to file motions, also the books will give a good understanding of available options for those not knowing where to start a case.

Wisconsin Law

	Chronological Collection	Topical Collection
Statutes:	Wisconsin Acts, (Wis. Act)	WI Statutes (Wis. Stats.).
Administrative:	Administrative Register (Wis. Admin. Code)	WI Administrative Code (Wis. Adm. Code) End.
Case Law:	Callahan's Wisconsin Reporter (Wis., Wis.2d) Official	
	Northwestern Reporter (N.W., N.W.2d) Non-official	

WI Acts (session laws, 2011 WI Act #) are created by the legislature and codified into statutes. **Wisconsin Statutes** are bound laws according to their subject. They can be found at: https://docs.legis.wisconsin.gov/statutes/prefaces/toc. Utilize the **Wisconsin Statute Annotated** to find the West Key # in the West Wisconsin Key Digest and reference to case law. Use the two volume books of the **General Index to the WI Annotated** to find statutes relating to subject. Words and phrases and the general index are located in the last volume of WI state statutes.

Administrative codes are passed by agencies of the government and codified into the **Wisconsin Administrative Code** by subject.

Each county in Wisconsin has a District or Circuit Court. Appellate courts have 16 judges and divided into four districts (Madison, Milwaukee, Waukesha and Wausau). The Wisconsin Supreme Court is located in Madison.

West publishing has a volume of books called **West WI Key # Digest**. This set of books utilizes three indexes which consist of: 1. Descriptive words 2. Words and phrases 3. Tables and cases (can look up case names). Once the subject and key # is found look up the subject in the main digest along with the key (think of the key as section). These keys can find their way into statute and case law.

Wisconsin Shepard's Citators are used to "Shepardize" law. Different volumes exist for state, federal, regional, and other special related topics. Case law can be looked up by domain citation, name, or case law citation. Statutes are also shepardized (history notes, acts, and case law relating to statute). Underneath the citations are case history, parallel citation in parenthesis and all related cases involving that same subject which is listed under that citation. A table of abbreviations exists in the beginning of each volume to understand case history and treatment. Shepardizing terminology is owned by Lexis so if you are using Westlaw use the Keycite feature.

Example of Shepardizing Case Law

1. Find the case name and citation in Shepard's books.

2. Below the citation number is the case, year decided and then the parallel citation in parentheses. Parallel citation is the same case published in an unofficial reporter.

3. Case history and related cases are given below the parallel citations.

Examples:

2001 WI 59	Case
Wis.Prof'l	*
Police Ass'n v	*
Lightbourn	*
2001	*
(243Wis2d512)	Citation
(627NW2nd807)	Parallel Citation
US cert den	
534US1080	
US cert den	
151LE2nd696	

2006 WI 13	
Progressive N.	
Ins. Co. v Hall	
2006	
(288Wis2d282)	
(709NW2d46)	
s 2005 WI App 17	(s) same case

2005 WI APP 17	
Progressive N.	
Ins. Co. v Hall	
(278Wis2d499)	
(692NW2d355)	
Gr 2005WI134	(Gr) granted
a 2006WI13	(a) affirmed

Shepard's case history abbreviations:

*   a = affirmed
*   cc = connected case
*   m = modified
*   D = dismissed
*   p = parallel
*   r = reversed
*   s = same case
*   S = superseded
*   v = vacated

Shepard's Case treatment abbreviations
- c = criticized
- d = distinguished
- e = explained
- f = followed
- j = dissenting
- L = limited
- ~ = concurring
- o = overruled
- q = questioned
- su = superseded by statute

Check yellow (yearly) and red (monthly) supplements for updates to the cases or statutes.

Example of Shepardizing Statute

Example:

943.207	Statute
Ad 1975c300	(Ad) Added
A 1999 Act 51	
91Wis2d499	
283NW2nd621	
Subsec. 1	
A 1999Act 51	(A) Amended
Subd. C	
Ad 1999Act 51	
Subsec. 2	
A&Rn 943	(A&Rn) Added and Renumbered

Books shown below are available at the Fox Valley Technical College Library, Appleton WI.

1. United States Code Service
2. U.S. Supreme Court Digest
3. Federal Reporter
4. American Law Reports – with index
5. West's legal forms
6. WI Jury Instructions: Civil and Criminal
7. North West Reporter
8. Wisconsin Pleadings & Practice

Case Content

General appealed case layout:

1. Parties involved
2. Court level
3. Docket number & year of decision
4. Parallel citation
5. Head note (do not quote)
6. Trial court judge
7. Author of opinion
8. Procedural history
9. Issue
10. Holding
11. Facts
12. Disposition (reversed, remanded etc...)
13. Dissention (disagreement)

Note: All judges are presumed to be in the majority unless otherwise notation of judges in dissention or absence is found.

State Case Citations

All states are bound into and published into seven regions called <u>Regional Reporters:</u> <u>A.2d</u> Atlantic Reporter, <u>N.E.2d</u> Northeastern Reporter, <u>N.W.2d</u> Northwestern Reporter (Wisconsin), <u>P.2d</u> Pacific Reporter, <u>S.E.2d</u> Southeastern Reporter, <u>So.2d</u> Southern Reporter, <u>S.W.2d</u> Southwestern Reporter. Each state has their proprietary set of reports. WI is called Wisconsin Reports. Citations are formed by utilizing a book called <u>The Bluebook – A Uniform System of Citation</u> 19th Edition.

Both the Wisconsin Supreme Court and the Wisconsin Court of Appeals are published in two books. One is official and the other is non-official.
1. Callaghan's Wisconsin Reporter (Wis., Wis.2d) (official *).
2. Northwestern Reporter N.W., N.W.2d (non-official **).

Typical Case Law Citation: <u>Andrews v. Ryan, 123 Wis. 2d 78, 198 N.W. 2d 911 (1992).</u>

$$\quad 1 \qquad\qquad 2 \qquad\qquad 3 \qquad\qquad 4$$

1. Andrews v. Ryan: Plaintiff v. Defendant.
2. 123 Wis. 2d 78: Volume 123, Callaghan's Wisconsin Reporter, page 78.
3. 198 N.W. 2d 911: Volume 198, Northwestern Reporter (2nd edition), page 911.
4. 1992: Year published.

Typical Case Law Citation: <u>ABC Corp. v. Geico Ins.</u>, 2000 WI APP 78, 211 Wis. 2d 8, 300 N.W.2d 150.   (See note)

Note: 2000 WI APP 78: After January 1st, 2000 all WI cases have a computer domain citation that states the year, reporter, and case number after the parties.

State cases in state courts: Rule 10.3.1 "Citations to the official state reporter followed by a parallel citation to a regional reporter" (The Bluebook – A Uniform System of Citation, 19th Edition.). Example: Plaintiff v. Defendant, Public Domain (year, state, appeals, case #), Official Reporter, Regional Reporter (100 is volume of book and 10 is page number start). After certain dates, requirements for a domain citation exist. Domain is year of case, state decided and case # of the year which appears before the reporters in citations. No domain citation exists in federal cases. Case citations referenced from The Bluebook – A Uniform System of Citation 19th Edition. Look up cases in table T1: Federal p.215, States p.228
State cases in their state Court:

Smith v. Jones, 100 Wis.2d 10, 100 N.W.2d 10 (1999). (WI Rep. 2nd edition, Regional Rep. 2nd edition, year of case).

Smith v. Jones, 100 Wis.2d 10, 100 N.W.2d 10 (Ct.App. 1999). (WI Rep., Regional Rep., Appeals court).

Smith v. Jones, 2011 WI 6, 100 Wis.2d 10, 100 N.W.2d 10. (P.D. (Year, state, case order), State Rep., Regional Rep.).

Smith v. Jones, 2011 WI APP 6, 100 Wis.2d 10, 100 N.W.2d 10. (P.D. (Year, state, case order), State Rep., Regional Rep.).

Smith v. Jones, 2011 Pa. 203, 100 Pa. 10, 100 A.2d 10. (P.D., State Rep., Regional Rep.).

Smith v. Jones, 2011 Pa. Super 203, 100 Pa. 10, 100 A.2d 10. (P.D. (appeals), State Rep., Regional Rep.).

Smith v. Jones, 100 Tenn.App 10, 100 S.W.3d 10 (2011).

Smith v. Jones, 100 N.Y.2d 10, 100 N.E.2d 10 (2011).

State cases outside their state Court: Rule 10.3.1 (b) "In all other documents…, cite the relevant regional rep." (The Bluebook – A Uniform System of Citation 19th Ed.).

Smith v. Jones, 100 N.W.2d 10 (Wis. 1999).

Smith v. Jones, 100 N.W.2d 10 (Wis.Ct.App. 1996).

Smith v. Jones, 2011 WI 6, 100 N.W.2d 10.

Smith v. Jones, 2011 Pa. 203, 100 A.2d 10.

Smith v. Jones, 100 A.2d 10 (PA 1985). (No Domain in older cases).

<u>Smith v. Jones</u>, 2011 Pa. 203, 100 A.2d 10 (Super.Ct.).

<u>Smith v. Jones</u>, 100 So.3d 10 (Fla. Dist.Ct.App.2011).

<u>Smith v. Jones,</u> 100 P.3d 10 (Haw. 2011).

<u>Smith v. Jones</u>, 100 N.W.2d (Minn. 2011).

<u>Smith v. Jones</u>, 100 N.E.2d 10 (Ill.App.Ct. 1999).

<u>Smith v. Jones</u>, 100 A.2d 10 (Md. 2011).

<u>The Bluebook – A Uniform System of Citation</u> 19th Edition.

10.2 Case Names   page 89

10.3 Citations   page 95

10.4 Jurisdiction   page 98

10.5 Year   page 99

12 Statutes   page 114-115 12.3.1 bd & 12.3.2

Regional Reporters

Atlantic Reporter: Connecticut, Maine, New Hampshire, Rhode Island, Vermont, Delaware, New Jersey, DC Maryland, Pennsylvania

North Eastern Region: Ohio, Indiana, Illinois, New York, Massachusetts

North Western Reporter: Iowa, Michigan, Minnesota, Nebraska, North Dakota, South Dakota, Wisconsin

Southern Reporter: Louisiana, Alabama, Florida, Mississippi

South Eastern Reporter: North Carolina, South Carolina, West Virginia, Virginia, Georgia

South Western Reporter: Arkansas, Missouri, Kentucky, Tennessee, Texas

Pacific Reporter: Alaska, Arizona, California, Colorado, Hawaii, Idaho, Montana, Nevada, Oregon, Utah, Washington, Wyoming, New Mexico, Kansas, Oklahoma

Law Citations

68 Am. Jur. 2d <u>Search and Seizure</u> § 285 (year).   Rule 15, Page 144

26 A. L. R. 5th 245 (year).   American Law Reports

76 C. J. S. <u>Landlord and Tenant</u> § 84 (year).   Rule 15, Page 144

47 U. S. C. A. § 315(b) (LexisNexis year).   Non official - cite book used

I. R. C. § 3022 (B) (3) (year).   Rule 14, Page 133

I. R. C. §§ 315-320 (B) (3) (year).   Rule 12, Page 111

I. R. C. § 320 (B) (3) (Supp. | 1983).   Rule 12 (e), Page 115

Model Land Dev. Code § 2-706 (year).   Rule 12, Page 122

Wis. JI-Crim 1185 (year).

Wis. Stat. § 346.11 (2009-10).

Wis. Stat. Ann. § 346.11(West year).   Non official - cite book used

Wis. Admin. Code § DE 2.01 (year).

Wis. Admin. Code § Tour 1.03 (year).

<u>West's Legal Forms</u> § 18:45 (2008).

<u>Wis. Pleading § Practice</u> § 20:97 (2009).

If a case is not available in print, state the name of case, the docket #, online reporter citation, name of court and exact date of decision. Do not cite unpublished cases.

Federal Law

Federal laws are passed by Congress and bound in volumes called Statutes at Large (Stat). The Statutes are codified into 50 titles called the United States Code (U.S.C.) by subject matter. Agencies of the Federal Government issue administrative codes and print them in the Federal Register (Fed. Reg.). These codes are compiled into the Code of Federal Regulation (C.F.R.) by subject matter. Wisconsin has an Eastern and Western District Court. The Appeals Circuit is Chicago 7th Circuit and the Supreme Court is in Washington D.C.

Federal Law

	Chronological	Topical
Statutes:	Statutes at Large (Stat.)	United States Code (U.S.C.)
Administrative:	Federal Register (Fed. Reg.).	Code of Federal Regulations (C.F.R.) End.

National Cites for federal and state law

1. Law.cornell.edu: USC, CFR
2. Washlaw.edu
3. GPO.gov.fdsys: (Federal Digital System)
4. Thomas.loc.gov: (Thomas Law Library) Links to Senate, House of Reps., legislation, bills, etc.
5. Findlaw.com: Find lawyers, legal forms, and topics.
6. Megalaw.com
7. Allaboutforms.com: Free legal forms.
8. Law.cornell.edu/rules/frcp/: Federal Court Rules

For a more in-depth understanding of administrative rules, see Administrative Law Review Volume 64, Number 3, summer 2012, 64 Admin. L. Rev. 565 (2012) titled "Administrative Law Through the Lens of Immigration Law".

Federal Case Citations

Federal case law consists of the U.S. Supreme Court, The U.S. Court of Appeals and U.S. District Courts. U.S. District Courts reside inside the states and U.S. Court of Appeals has states grouped together into eleven regions. For example: The U.S. Court of Appeals for the 7th District is Wisconsin, Indiana and Illinois. Wisconsin has an Eastern and Western Federal District Court. Www.supremecourtus.gov provides daily coverage of Supreme Court cases. www.uscourts.gov posts federal cases.

Federal Courts utilize a book called Federal Rules of Civil Procedure (FRCP) which can be found at www.law.cornell.edu/rules/frcp/. A Federal Civil Rules Handbook exists to guide your way through the FRCP along with the Federal Rules of Evidence book. When litigating in a Wisconsin Federal Court FRCP has been incorporated into a book called Wisconsin Court Rules and Procedure – Federal. Use the book Federal Criminal Code and Rules for federal criminal procedure.

The U.S. Supreme Court decisions are published identically into three books.
1. United States Reports U.S. (official).
2. Supreme Court Reporter S. Ct. (unofficial).
3. Lawyer's Edition L. Ed (unofficial).

Typical Case Law Citation: Smith V. Jones, 520 U.S. 30, 110 S. Ct. 782, 92 L.Ed.2d 1112 (1995).   1   2   3   4

5

1. Smith V. Jones: Plaintiff V. Defendant.
2. 520 U.S. 30: Volume 520, U.S. Reports, Page 30.
3. 110 S. Ct. 782: Volume 110, Supreme Court Reporter, Page 782.
4. 92 L.Ed.2d 1112: Volume 92, Lawyers Edition (2nd), Page 1112.
5. 1995: Year published.

The U.S. Circuit Court of Appeals is published into the Federal Reporter.
Typical Case Law Citation: Johnson v. Adams, 888 F.2d 90 (7th Cir. 1990).
      1   2   3

1. Smith V. Jones: Plaintiff v. Defendant.
2. 888 F.2d 90: Volume 888, Federal Reporter (2nd edition), Page 90.
3. 7th Cir. 1990: Seventh Circuit published 1990.

The U.S. District Court gets published into the Federal Supplement.

Typical Case Law Citation: Brady v. Johnson, 79 F.Supp. 378 (W.D. Wis. 1952).

1. Brady v. Johnson: Plaintiff v. Defendant

2. 79 F.Supp 378: Volume 79, Federal Supplement, page 378.

3. W.D. Wis. 1952: Western District, Wisconsin, published 1952.

■■■

U.S. Supreme Court Federal Case Reports: US Rep. (official), Supreme Court Rep., Lawyer's Ed.

Smith v. Jones, 100 U.S. 10, 100 S.Ct 10, 100 L.Ed.2d 10 (2011).

U.S. Court of Appeals (WI 7th District): Federal Rep. F., F.2d, F.3d.

Smith v. Jones 100 F.2d 10 (7th Cir. 1990).

Smith v. Jones, 802 F.2d 319 (11th Cir. 1986).

U.S. District Court: F.Supp., F.Supp.2d.

Smith v. Jones, 100 F.Supp. 10 (W.D. Wis. 1952). (Western Federal District of WI).

Smith v. Jones, 100 F.Supp.2d 10 (E.D. KY. 2011).

Smith v. Jones, 100 F.Supp.2d 10 (S.D. Tex. 2000).

Federal Circuits

Federal Circuit (Washington)

D.C. Circuit (Washington): District of Columbia

1st Circuit (Boston): Maine, Massachusetts, New Hampshire, Puerto Rico, Rhode Island

2nd Circuit (New York): Connecticut: Connecticut, New York, Vermont

3rd Circuit (Philadelphia): Delaware, New Jersey, Pennsylvania, U.S. Virgin Islands

4th Circuit (Richmond): Maryland, North Carolina, South Carolina, Virginia, West Virginia

5th Circuit (New Orleans): Louisiana, Mississippi, Texas

6th Circuit (Cincinnati): Kentucky, Michigan, Ohio, Tennessee

7th Circuit (Chicago): Illinois, Indiana, Wisconsin

8th Circuit (St. Louis): Arkansas, Iowa, Minnesota, Missouri, Nebraska, North Dakota, South Dakota

9th Circuit (San Francisco): Alaska, Arizona, California, Guam, Hawaii, Idaho, Montana, Nevada, Northern Mariana Islands, Oregon, Washington.

10th Circuit (Denver): Colorado, Kansas, New Mexico, Oklahoma, Utah, Wyoming

11th Circuit (Atlanta): Alabama, Florida, Georgia

Criminal Liability

Actus Reus: a wrongful act or omission. Often defined as various elements in statutes.

Mens Rea: a wrongful mental state – the intent to commit a wrongful act or omission. Purposely, knowingly, recklessly and negligent.

A. Strict Liability: Guilt without intent, exception to common law requirement of evil mind or act.

B. Malum in Se: Evil crime.

C. Malum Prohibitum: Only criminal due to declaration by legislation.

D. Transferred Intent: Unintended illegal act stemming from the intent to commit a crime is also a crime.

E. Vicarious Liability: Legal responsibility for actions of another person due to relationship (Corporate liability).

1st degree intentional (Death of another (actus reus)) intent to kill (Reus).

2nd Reckless Homicide (disregard for human life).

2nd degree intentional (Can't prove 1st degree).

2nd degree Reckless (heat of passion).

Negligent animal, weapon, explosives or firearms, intoxicated use of a vehicle, negligent operation of vehicle.

Theft:

1. Larceny : deprive of one's property.
2. Robbery: Threat or force.
3. Burglary: Intent to enter without consent to steal (felony).

Bribery:

1. Making a bribe.
2. Taking a Bribe.

Classification of Crimes

Felony: A serious crime that may result in >1 year in prison and has a six year statute of limitation.

Misdemeanor: less serious crimes that may result in up to 1 year in jail with a statute of limitation of three years.

Petty Offenses: mostly code violations and minor traffic offenses.

Defenses (Intent-based):

1. Insanity: Diminished capacity & irresistible impulse.
2. Duress: necessity.
3. Mistake.
4. Statute of Limitations.
5. Mistaken Identity.

Alibi: Must be notice of Alibi sent to the state 30 days prior to trial for state to check them out.

Criminal definitions:

Alford plea: judgment of conviction entered; defendant maintains innocence claim.

Arraignment: Defendant is read the formal charge.

Assault: Force.

Battery: Intentional touching.

Due Process Model: Individual rights over rights of community.

Miranda v. Arizona: Must inform suspects of their rights before interrogation. Evidence obtained in violation of Miranda is subject to the exclusionary rule, and cannot be used during trial.

No contest: judgment of conviction entered; no admission of guilt.

Plea Bargain: exchange of charges or sentence recommendation for a guilty/no contest plea.

Probable Cause: substantial likelihood that, if a crime was committed, the defendant did it.

Reasonable Suspicion: A standard of proof that is less than probable cause to detain a person if they believe or have a suspicion that a crime has been or is about to be committed. It is generally short of a probable cause to arrest. An officer may frisk a person (pat down) or vehicle for weapons for officer safety only. This act is also known as a Terry stop. Under the plain feel doctrine if contraband is clearly felt during a frisk, it may be seized. The plain feel will convert to a new probable cause.

Retreat Doctrine: The duty to retreat if a defendant is to prove that his or her conduct was justified in defending themselves.

Plain View Doctrine: Allows an officer to seize without warrant evidence in plain view during a lawful observation.

Warrant: an order, based on probable cause, allowing an arrest or search of premises.

Wis.Stat.Ann. § 939.51 (2011)

(1) Misdemeanors in chs. 939 to 951 are classified as follows:

(3) Penalties for misdemeanors are as follows:

(a) For a Class A misdemeanor, a fine not to exceed $10,000 or imprisonment not to exceed 9 months, or both.

(b) For a Class B misdemeanor, a fine not to exceed $1,000 or imprisonment not to exceed 90 days, or both.

(c) For a Class C misdemeanor, a fine not to exceed $500 or imprisonment not to exceed 30 days, or both.

Wis.Stat.Ann. § 939.50 (2011)

(3) Penalties for felonies are as follows:

(a) For a Class A felony, life imprisonment (Example: Homicide).

(b) For a Class B felony, imprisonment not to exceed 60 years (Example: Rape).

(c) For a Class C felony, a fine not to exceed $ 100,000 or imprisonment not to exceed 40 years, or both.

(d) For a Class D felony, a fine not to exceed $ 100,000 or imprisonment not to exceed 25 years, or both.

(e) For a Class E felony, a fine not to exceed $ 50,000 or imprisonment not to exceed 15 years, or both.

(f) For a Class F felony, a fine not to exceed $25,000 or imprisonment not to exceed 12 years and 6 months, or both.

(g) For a Class G felony, a fine not to exceed $25,000 or imprisonment not to exceed 10 years, or both.

(h) For a Class H felony, a fine not to exceed $10,000 or imprisonment not to exceed 6 years, or both.

(i) For a Class I felony, a fine not to exceed $10,000 or imprisonment not to exceed 3 years and 6 months, or both.

Over ninety percent of the false convictions of rape exonerations were based on eyewitness misidentification. See the movie *"After Innocence"* 2005.
Memory is dynamic;- this means that it changes. Memory is not stored in the human brain like a computer, it can be induced. This is how false confessions are created.

Expungement of record can be asked for on H felony and lower; however, it must be asked for at original sentencing.

Pretrial Motions: Motion for Bill of Particulars, dismiss, quash, suppress, change of venue and motion in limine (evidence admitted or struck).

Defendant has a right to a jury trial when there is more than six months' punishment. A breathalyzer is not enough to prove intoxication in court; however it is probable cause for a blood test to move forward. A probable cause to pullover a vehicle can convert to a new probable cause.

Louisiana is the only state not bound to common law. This state was a French territory and is bound to civil law, making legislative code primary.

The State can hold a suspect 48 hours until bond set or hearing.

Citizen arrest is for felony only.

Entrapment must be encouraged for it to be valid.

Civil Suit Overview
WI Stats 801

1. Accident, breach of contract or other event.
2. Consultation with attorney.
3. Informal investigation.
4. Plaintiff's attorney files complaint.
5. Defendant notified of Lawsuit: Summons and complaint served if service not waived.
6. Defendant's attorney files answer to complaint or motion to dismiss.
7. Motion for judgment on the pleadings (request to end based on information).
8. Discovery.
9. Motion for summary judgment (request to end based on information).
10. Further discovery.
11. Pretrial Conference.
12. Jury selection.
13. Trial.
14. Post trial motions.
15. Appeal.
16. Steps to enforce and collect judgment.

Summons: Notifies person that they are being sued. Complaint is the allegations. Get courthouse copies, have sheriff or service serve. Proof is required. Affidavit of service. $50 to 100 per attempt.

Discovery:
1. Interrogatories: Opposing parties only, questions/written request.
2. Deposition: Anyone, court reporter.
3. Request for production of documents: (gets stuff).
4. Request for admission.

Things (speech) not discoverable:
1. Husband/wife.
2. Doctor/patient.

3. Clergyman

Pretrial motions:

1. Motion to dismiss.

2. Motion to strike.

3. Motion to make more definite statement.

4. Motion for judgment on the pleadings.

5. Motion to compel discovery.

6. Motion for summary judgment.

7. Motion to amend a pleading.

8. Motion for change of venue.

9. Motion to quash return of service.

10. Motion for sanctions.

11. Motion In Limine (includes or excludes evidence away from the jury).

Post trial Motions:

1. Motion for a new trial.

2. Relief from judgment or order based on mistake, fraud etc...

Wis.Stat.Ann. § 893 covers "Statute of limitations".

Wisconsin Court Rules and Procedure book defines state court procedure and Wisconsin Court Rules and Procedure Local is used for individual counties.

STATE OF WISCONSIN   CIRCUIT COURT   WINNEBAGO COUNTY

GOOFY L. MCFERGUSSEN
    Plaintiff,

vs.

CHENEY TINKLESON,   Case No.: 280-CV-2020
ABC INSURANCE COMPANY
    Defendants.

NOTICE OF MOTION

To: Bruce Lee

        Attorney for Cheney Tinkleson and ABC Insurance Company

        111 East Street

        Neenah, WI 54956

PLEASE TAKE NOTICE that on October 25th, 2012 at 10:50 a.m. or as soon as the case will be called, the plaintiff by his attorney Daniel Huffinton will appear in room A125 of the Winnebago County Courthouse and present a Motion to the Court for a change of venue from Winnebago County Court to Outagamie County Court.

Dated this __14th__ of October, 2012.

                        Daniel Huffinton,
                        Attorney for the Plaintiff

                        By: _____
                        Daniel Huffington
                        State bar No. xoxoxo

STATE OF WISCONSIN   CIRCUIT COURT   WINNEBAGO COUNTY

GOOFY L. MCFERGUSSEN
Plaintiff,

vs.

CHENEY TINKLESON,   Case No.: 298-CV-2020
ABC INSURANCE COMPANY
Defendants.

MOTION FOR CHANGE OF VENUE

Plaintiff Goofy L. Mcfergussen by his attorney Daniel Huffinton moves the court for a change of venue to Outagamie County Circuit Court.

In Support of this motion, the plaintiff states:

1. It would be more convenient for both parties to adjudicate this matter in a court that is more convenient in distance and travel time.
2. The same justice will occur whether the case is heard in Outagamie or Winnebago County Court.
3. There will be no adverse consequences to the defendant for the change of venue.

WHEREFORE, plaintiff Goofy L. Mcfergussen requests the Court to enter an order changing the venue of the case.

Dated this 14th of October, 2012.

Daniel Huffington
Attorney for the Plaintiff
By: _____
Daniel Huffington
State bar No. Xoxoxo

STATE OF WISCONSIN   CIRCUIT COURT   WINNEBAGO COUNTY

GOOFY L. MCFERGUSSEN
    Plaintiff,

                                              Affidavit of Service

vs.

CHENEY TINKLESON,   Case No.: 95-CV-2012
ABC INSURANCE COMPANY
    Defendants.

State of Wisconsin

County of Winnebago

           I Daniel Huffinton, being first duly sworn, depose and say:

1. I am the attorney for the plaintiff in the above action.
2. A copy of the Motion and Notice of Motion for Change of Venue was served on the defendant on October 12th, 2012, and the return of service of Joe Jimmy, is on file in this action.

Dated this __14th__ of October, 2012.

                                     Daniel Huffinton,

                                     Attorney for the Plaintiff

                                     By: _____

                                     Daniel Huffinton

                                     State bar No. 1003601

Example Affidavit

I Mr. Hicklehoppenhooper declare as follows.

1. I am over the age of eighteen years and am legally competent to make this declaration. I have personal knowledge of the facts contained herein. If called upon, I could and would competently under oath testify as to the facts stated herein.
2. I was at a certain location in Wisconsin.
3. I witnessed a robbery at a Piggly Wiggly grocery store.
4. I witnessed the robber get into a Chevrolet wagon.

I Mr. Hicklehoppenhooper hereby state that the facts above are true and correct to the best of my knowledge, information and belief. I further declare the statements above under penalty of perjury under the laws of the United States and the state of Wisconsin.

In witness whereof, I have hereunto set my hand and seal this _____ day of

_____

                                        _____

                                          Mr. Hicklehoppenhooper

Subscribed and sworn before me

This _____ day of _____, 20_____

_____
                     Name

Notary Public, State of Wisconsin

My Commission expires _____

State Court Complaint

1. Title establishing parties with case number, county branch and parties involved. Address on title can be dropped after original complaint.

2. Establish the court's jurisdiction over the parties by naming the parties and addresses.

3. Establish a "set of facts". One set of facts per line.

4. Wherefore & signature block. Wherefore does not ask for a dollar amount in a tort.

5. A summons is used to notify the defendant of the complaint. WI Statute section 801.095 for a summons form. Federal complaints must use a coversheet and summons downloadable at www.wied.uscourts.gov

****

STATE OF WISCONSIN	CIRCUIT COURT BRANCH	WINNEBAGO COUNTY

GOOFY L. MCFERGUSSEN
952 Starlight Avenue
Neenah, WI 54956
Plaintiff,

      vs.

	Case Number:	09 CV____
	Case Code:	30703

CHENEY TINKLESON LLC,
853 Ziplock Street
Neenah, WI 54956
ABC INSURANCE COMPANY
Defendants.

COMPLAINT

NOW COMES THE Plaintiff Goofy Mcfergussen by his Attorney Daniel Huffington and as for causes of action against the Defendant, Cheney Tinkleson, hereby alleges, and shows to the Court, as follows:

1. Plaintiff Goofy L. Mcfergussen is an adult resident of 952 Starlight Avenue in Neenah, Winnebago County, Wisconsin.

2. Upon information and belief, the Defendant, Cheney Tinkleson LLC, (hereinafter "Tinkleson") is a domestic limited liability company organized under the laws of the State of Wisconsin engaged primarily in the business of home construction, with the principal offices at 853 Ziplock Street in Neenah

Wisconsin. The registered agent for service of process for Cheney Tinkleson LLC is Cheney Tinkleson at the same address.

3. The involuntary plaintiff ABC Insurance Company is an insurance company authorized to do business in the State of Wisconsin and insurer of Cheney Tinkleson LLC.

4. On or about, June 25, 2012 the Plaintiff and Defendant entered into a contract for improvements to the Plaintiff's home to be completed by Defendant. A true and correct copy of said contract is attached hereto and incorporated herein by reference as Exhibit "A".

First Cause of Action
Breach of Contract

5. That on or about, June 30, 2012 the Defendant began the agreed renovations to the Plaintiff's home.

6. That on or about, July 12, 2012 the Defendant completed the work on the Plaintiff's home for a price of $17,000.00

7. That on or about, July 21, 2012 the Plaintiff noticed a rippled kitchen floor which was caused by water saturation.

8. That on or about, July 22, 2012 the Plaintiff hired Housing Repair Specialist to repair the water damaged floor.

9. That on or about, July 30, 2012 Housing Repair Specialist completed the damaged home repairs for $102,000.00

10. That to date, the water damage was caused by a pierced water line during the installation of kitchen cupboards.

11. That to date, the cause of water damage was a direct result of negligent installation of Kitchen cupboards by the Defendant Tinkleson.

12. That the Defendant failed to exercise ordinary care in the remodelling of the Plaintiff's home.

WHEREFORE, the plaintiff Goofy Mcfergussen, demands judgment against the defendant of $102,000.00 plus interest, together with costs, disbursements, attorney fees, and such other relief as the Court deems appropriate.

Dated this ___ day of September, 2012.

_____

Daniel Huffington

Attorney for the Plaintiff

State Bar No.: _____

MAILING ADDRESS:

1616 Lowrance Street

****

Example of a wherefore demand in at tort case

WHEREFORE, the plaintiff Goofy Mcfergussen, demands judgment against the defendant:

A. In the amount of to be determined by the court to compensate her for the additional costs and expenses in correcting the negligent construction for the Defendant; and

B. Costs, disbursements, attorney fees, and such other relief as the Court deems appropriate.

Note: In a breach of contract use the "Unjust Enrichment" in the set of facts.

Unjust Enrichment: is where one person is unjustly or by chance enriched at the expense of another, and an obligation to make restitution arises, regardless of liability for wrongdoing.

STATE OF WISCONSIN   CIRCUIT COURT   WINNEBAGO COUNTY

BRANCH

GOOFY L. MCFERGUSSEN
     Plaintiff,

vs.

CHENEY TINKLESON,
ABC INSURANCE COMPANY   Case No.: 95-CV-2012
     Defendants.

ANSWER

COME NOW the defendants, Cheney Tinkleson and ABC Insurance Company by their attorney Bruce Lee and as for an Answer to the Complaint of the Plaintiff, allege and show to the Court as follows:

1. With reference to Paragraph 1 of the Plaintiff's Complaint, these answering defendants admit the allegations.
2. With reference to Paragraph 2 of the Plaintiff's Complaint, these answering defendants admit the allegations.
3. With reference to Paragraph 3 of the Plaintiff's Complaint, these answering defendants admit the allegations.
4. With reference to Paragraph 4 of the Plaintiff's Complaint, these answering defendants admit that "Goofy L. Mcfergussen hired Cheney Tinkleson the defendant to install new kitchen cupboards at Mcfergussen's residence of 952 Fairview Avenue, Neenah. These defendants deny that "During the cupboard installation the screws used to mount the cupboard pierced a water line routed inside the wall. This ruptured line seeped into the wall and underneath the kitchen floor. As a result a new sub floor and tiling had to be replaced."
5. With reference to Paragraph 5 of the Plaintiff's Complaint, these answering defendants deny being negligent in the installation of cupboards creating damage to the flooring.

6. With reference to Paragraph 6 of the Plaintiff's Complaint, these answering defendants deny the allegations based on no actual knowledge of any work being done on the house from LLC Specialist.

REQUEST FOR RELIEF

WHEREFORE, these answering defendants pray for judgment:

1. Dismissing the complaint of the plaintiff on its merits.
2. For the costs and disbursements incurred in this action.
3. For such further and equitable relief as the Court may deem appropriate.

Dated this _8th_ of October, 2012.

Bruce Lee
Attorney for the Defendants

By:_____
Bruce Boy
State bar No. xoxoxox

STATE OF WISCONSIN CIRCUIT COURT WINNEBAGO COUNTY

GOOFY L. MCFERGUSSEN
      Plaintiff,

vs.

CHENEY TINKLESON,   Case No.: 95-CV-2012
ABC INSURANCE COMPANY
      Defendants.

TO: Bruce Lee, Attorney of Record for Defendant, Cheney Tinkleson and ABC
            Insurance Company, in the above styled and numbered cause.

            Pursuant to Rule 34 of the Federal Rules of Civil Procedure, Goofy L.
Mcfergussen, plaintiff in the above cause, requests that Cheney
Tinkleson, defendant in the above cause, produce for inspection and
copying by December, within thirty days of service hereof or at such
other time as may be agreed upon by counsel for the parties, originals
or legible copies of the documents and electronically stored
information in the formats specified below requested herein. You are
also requested to serve upon plaintiff within thirty (30) days after
service of the request a written response in accordance with Rule 34 of
the Federal Rules of Civil Procedure.

DOCUMENTS REQUESTED

1. A request of the original signed agreement of the work estimate used to start remodelling on the house of Goofy L. Mcfergussen.

2. A list of the employee work schedules at the time that work on Goofy L. Mcfergussen house was being completed. Only the work schedules of those that did work on that particular house need to be included.

3. A copy of the personal file that was used during the entire work and or communication between Goofy L. Mcfergussen and Cheney Tinkleson.

4. An itemized bill stating exactly what was done and billed after all the work had been completed at Goofy L. Mcfergussen's house.

5. A copy of the payment or verification made at the end of work completion.

Dated this _15th_ of November, 2012.

> Daniel Huffington
> Attorney for the Plaintiff
> By:_____
> Daniel Huffington
> State bar No. xoxoxo1

Note: A Request for documents is part of the discovery process of a lawsuit.

STATE OF WISCONSIN   CIRCUIT COURT   WINNEBAGO COUNTY

GOOFY L. MCFERGUSSEN
    Plaintiff,

vs.

CHENEY TINKLESON,   Case No.: 95-CV-2012
ABC INSURANCE COMPANY
    Defendants.

INTERROGATORY

Pursuant to rule 805, of Wisconsin Court Rules and Procedure, you are to answer the interrogatories hereinafter set forth, separately, fully, in writing, and under oath. You should deliver a true copy of your answer to the undersigned attorney within 30 days after the date of service of these interrogatories.

INSTRUCTIONS

A.   You are required by rule 805 of the Wisconsin Court Rules and Procedure to:

    1.   Answer fully and factually each of the interrogatories hereinafter set out.

    2.   Furnish all information called for by said interrogatory.

    3.   Sign your response.

    4.   Swear to your response.

    5.   Serve same upon the undersigned attorney within (30) days after the date of service of these interrogatories. You are further instructed:

B.   Every interrogatory herein shall be deemed a continuing interrogatory, and you are to supplement your answers promptly if and when you obtain relevant information in addition to , or in any way inconsistent with, your initial answer to any interrogatory.

1. State the name of each and every employee that worked on the home of Goofy L. Mcfergussen.

2. State the experience of each of those individuals that you answered to in the previous question.

3. State the names of the individuals who installed the upper kitchen cabinets.

4. State the type of interview process used when hiring new employees.

Dated this _21st_ of October, 2012.

Daniel Huffington
Attorney for the Plaintiff
By:_____
Daniel Huffington
State bar No. xixi

Civil Trial Procedure

Jury selection is done the first day of court. The judge leads the courtroom during jury selection and swears in the jurors. The Clerk calls 23 possible jurors from the entire group. The judge questions the juries <u>Voir Dire</u> for prejudice or relation to the parties making sure jurors are impartial. The plaintiff gets to ask questions of jurors and then the defendant does also. Each attorney writes down (strikes) certain jurors to get the number down to 13. This will leave one extra juror. Some judges allow jurors to take notes and ask questions (in writing). These questions become exhibits. Civil trials outcomes depend on a preponderance of evidence (51% likely). In a civil case if the statute of limitations is three years and something is done to get the other party to recognize the issue (within the three years) an additional three years can be added from that point.

<u>Voir Dire</u>: A process of asking questions to reveal bias (to tell the truth).

<u>Peremptory challenge</u>: each side gets equal number of strikes, for any reason.

<u>Side Bar:</u> Lawyers meeting at judge's desk.

<u>Refresh recollection:</u> Provide witness with copy and witness reads.

<u>Objection:</u> Overruled: go ahead and answer. Sustained: rephrase or ask a different question.

Steps of a Trial:

1. Plaintiff's Opening Statement.
2. Defendant's Opening Statement.
3. Plaintiff's Case in Chief: Plaintiff calls witnesses; Defendant cross examines; Plaintiff redirects; Defendant recrosses.
4. Defendant's Case in Chief: Defendant calls witnesses; Plaintiff cross examines; Defendant redirects; Plaintiff recrosses.
5. Plaintiff's Closing Arguments.
6. Defendant's Closing Arguments.
7. Plaintiff's rebuttal.
8. Jury Instructions, Deliberation and Verdict.

The Appeal:

1. File notice of appeal
2. Court clerk compiles record
3. Attorneys file legal briefs
4. Appeals court may allow oral argument

Possible dispositions:

Affirm

Reverse

Remand

Wisconsin Jury Instructions

Two sets of **Wisconsin Jury Instructions** exist.
1. Criminal cited as: Wis. JI-Crim 1185 (year).
2. Civil

Select the set of books and review the table of contents to find the instructions for statutory violations.

Jury Instructions can be agreed upon by the judge and both opposing parties.

Land

Real Property: Land, buildings, fixtures (dishwasher etc.), trees.

Personal Property: Goods and crops not permanently affixed to land or buildings
1. Tangible: Movable and touchable. Example: Real property (Land, Trees, buildings, fixtures) and Personal property (ships, automobiles, tools etc.).
2. Intangible: Not movable or touchable: Example: Copyright, trademark, patents.

Property ownership:
1. Fee simple: single complete ownership, Tenancy in Severalty.
2. Concurrent ownership:
   a. Tenancy in Common: Co-ownership in real property (undivided). Right to use undivided whole. Interest passes to heirs at death. Tenancy in Common is default ownership in Wisconsin, WI Stats 700.18
   b. Joint Tenancy with the Right of Survivorship: By deed or will to own real property (undivided) as joint tenants; a deceased owner's interest will pass onto the surviving owner. Can sever if 1 sells his or her share or puts into a trust, would default new owner to a Tenancy in Common. Joint Tenancy must be created at the same time, have unity in title, equal interest in land, and right for each individual to possess entire property. Marriage by default is Joint Tenancy with the Right of Survivorship WI Stats 700.19
   c. Tenancy by the Entirety: From common law (Husband and Wife), neither can transfer without other's permission, treated as one owner. Right of Survivorship.
   d. Community Property: From Civil laws of Spain and France (Husband and Wife). It is statutory and property acquired during marriage is treated as equal. A few of the Community Property States: Arizona, California, New Mexico, Nevada, Idaho, Washington, Texas, Louisiana and Wisconsin.

Six types of Estates in Real Property:

1. Fee simple or fee simple absolute.
2. Fee simple determinable: Expires.
3. Fee simple on condition: Subsequent breach rescinds property.
4. Life estate: Expires on death, no probate, no creditors.
5. Estate for years: Owned for a period of time.
6. Estate at will: Indefinite period of time, an estate can be terminated at the will of the parties.

Land use:

1. Easements: right granted to a non owner of real property to use the real property for a specific purpose.
2. Prescriptive easements: Easement created when a person uses real property for a period without the owner's permission. Varies state to state, 10-20 years common for adverse possession.
3. Easement by necessity: Easement for access to a public street that is necessary for the use and enjoyment of the property being benefitted by the easement.

Real estate contract breach:

1. Specific performance: Court orders to perform contract.
2. Money damages: Money loss for contract not being performed.
3. Rescission: Remedy for default of real estate contract wherein the contract is terminated and the defaulting party must reimburse the injured party for expenses.
4. Liquidated damages: Amount agreed on by the parties to a contract to be paid in the event of a default.

Deeds: A written document that transfers ownership of real property from one person to another. Three main types of general warranty deeds exist.

1. General warranty deed: Depending on the state a general warranty deed will contain several covenants or warranties.
   A. Covenant of seisin: Grantor has full possession or title of the land.

B. Covenant of right to convey: Promise made by grantor that they own the land and have right to transfer.

C. Covenant against encumbrances: Promise that the land is not encumbered (tax lien, mortgage etc.).

D. Covenant of further assurance: Grantor will assure he agrees to satisfy any conditions so that the land conveyed is fee simple absolute.

E. Covenant of quiet enjoyment and warranty: Warranty to use the land without fear of third-party assertions of adverse claims.

2. Special warranty deed:

A. Where the grantor covenant and warrants only against the lawful claims of people claiming by, through or under the grantor.

3. Quitclaim Deed: Transfers only the interest the grantor has in the land and not the land itself. No covenants or warranties of title. Often found in foreclosures or executors of estates etc...

Valid deed contains:

1. Written.
2. Grantor.
3. Grantee.
4. Words of conveyance.
5. Adequate description of land.
6. Consideration: Something of value to make promises of contract enforceable.
7. Signature of Grantor.
8. Witness.
9. Delivery of deed to grantee.

Purchasing land or property in foreclosure:

1. Title company:

    A. Purchase a letter report from a title company. This will show the condition of the current ownership of that property and may show liens or unpaid property tax.
    B. Purchase a title commitment from a title company. This is the more expensive option; it is basically a promise that they will issue a title insurance policy.

2. Quitclaim will give interest in the property; a warranty deed warrants the title is marketable. A special warranty deed may be provided by the seller.

Estates

1. Administrator: A personal representative of an intestate estate, administratix if female.
2. Abatement: The process of determining the order in which gifts in a will are applied to debts and taxes.
3. Agent: A person authorized by another to act in place of the principal.
4. Ambulatory: A testator can change a will.
5. Apportionment clause: Tax allocation.
6. Attest: Verify a will as genuine.
7. Attorney in fact: An agent who is given authority by the principal in a written document called Power of Attorney. Does not need to be an attorney to be an agent.
8. Beneficiary: A person who receives property from a will.
9. Codicil: A written document to a will.
10. Devise/Devisee: Under probate code a person who receives a gift of personal or real property.
11. Domicile: Home
12. Durable power of attorney: Authorization to perform on behalf of principal.
13. Escheat: Transfer of property to the state when someone dies without a will or legal heirs.
14. Estate: What a person owns at death.
15. Execute: To write and sign a will.
16. Executor: A personal representative of a testate estate.
17. Freehold: Fee simple and life estate.
18. Heir: A person who receives property from an intestate estate.
19. Holographic will: Handwritten and signed by the testator.
20. Interrorem: Clause that punishes those who challenge the will by requiring forfeiture of the gift.
21. Inter vivos trust: A transfer or gift during one's lifetime.
22. Intestacy: Not having a will.
23. Leasehold: Tenancy for years.
24. Legatee: A person who receives property through a will.
25. Next of kin: A persons nearest blood relative.
26. Non-Probate: Joint and Community, pay on death, transfer to living trust and life insurance.
27. Nuncupative: Oral will.
28. Payable on death: P.O.D.
29. Per Capita: Heirs at the same generation will receive the same amount.
30. Per stirpes: Equal distribution of estate to relatives by representation.
31. Posthumous children: Born after death of testator.
32. Pretermitted children: Born after will.

33. Principal: A person who authorizes another to act on a person's behalf.
34. Pro Capita: Individual per person allowance of estate.
35. Probate: Real Property over 50k needs to be probated, no joint or community.
36. Self-proving: a will with an affidavit certifying the witnesses (for probate court).
37. Specific legacy: A specific gift by will.
38. Standing: A right to file a legal claim.
39. Subscribe: To sign a will as a witness.
40. Residuary Estate: After taxes.
41. Residuary clause: Assets distributed that are not directly allocated to specific individuals.
42. Reversionary interest: Right of the grantor to the return of real property after the termination of a life estate.
43. Testacy: Having a will.
44. Testamentary trust: Arises upon death.
45. Testator or Testatrix: Person who makes a will. Testatrix is a female making a will.
46. Transfer on death: T.O.D.
47. UPC: Uniform Probate Court.

Estate planning:
1. Trust if warranted.
2. Will.
3. Power of attorney for healthcare document.
4. Durable power of attorney.

Wills:
1. Introduction: Identify testator.
2. Revocation clause: Nulls other wills or codicils.
3. Provision for payment: Appoint personal representative for payment of debts and funeral expenses.
4. Instructions for burial.
5. Specific Testamentary gifts:
   a. Legacies: Gifts of money.
   b. Bequests: Gifts of personal property.
   c. Devises: Real property.

Power of Attorney:

A general power of attorney is a written document in which a principal appoints and authorizes an agent or attorney in fact to perform acts on behalf of the principal. A limited power of attorney is a written document in which an agent is appointed to do a limited amount of specific acts.

1. Nondurable (conventional) power of attorney starts when signed by the principal and lasts until a specific event occurs.
2. A durable power of attorney commences when signed by the principal and continues even if he becomes mentally incapacitated.
3. Springing power of attorney is tied to a specific event; it expires upon occurrence or death.

Four common grounds for contesting a will:

1. The language in will is not legal by law.
2. Lacked testamentary capacity to sign.
3. Testator influenced into signing.
4. The will is procured by fraud.

Ways to avoid probate:

1. Payable on death or transfer on death accounts.
2. Inter vivos trust.
3. Life Insurance payable on death.
4. Property owned in joint tenancy.

Probate steps:

1. Petition for probate.
2. Citation or interested party notice.
3. Intestate: Proving the will, self-proving will waived.
4. Bond by personal representative.
5. Court issues letters giving authority to make decisions on behalf of the deceased.
6. Inventory filed.
7. Notice to creditors.
8. Taxes and expenses are paid.
9. Distribution to beneficiaries.
10. Final account is filed in court.
11. Close estate.

Trusts

The National Conference of Commissioners on Uniform State Laws otherwise known as the Uniform Law Commission established in 1892 works on finding unity and harmony on many state laws. The Uniform Trust Code created by the ULC is adopted in 22 states.

A trust is formed when real or personal property is transferred from a settler to one or more trustees. A settler is the person who creates a trust also known as a donor or grantor and the trustee holds legal title to the property in a trust for the benefit of beneficiaries. A Trust Instrument is a written instrument that creates a trust. A beneficiary holds equitable title while the legal title is ownership of the trust property. A trust is created on paper and usually titled with the settlers name depending on what type of trust is created. For example: "Trust Agreement of "your name"". Then property is titled or transferred into that trust. The trust can hold property and can be transferred upon death of the settler if that's what the trust states to do. The settler can still hold other property outside of the trust and have a last will and testament to determine what to do with that part of the estate.

Intervivvos is a living trust:
      1. Revocable Trust: Can be sought after for personal debt.
      2. Irrevocable Trust: Cannot be sought after for debt.
Passive or Testamentary trust: is created upon passing of one's life.
Active trust: A settler gives powers and duties to the trustee. In a passive trust, the trustee has no duties to perform but holds the property for the beneficiary.
A resulting or constructive trust is considered an implied trust and created by operation of a court.

Business Operation

Sole Proprietorship

1. Unlimited personal liability.
2. No registration unless business name is different that the individual.
3. Pass through taxation.
4. One or more employees to form a Sole Proprietorship

Limited Liability Partnerships

1. Limited Partnership, Limited Liability Partnership, Limited Liability Limited Partnership.
2. Joint and Several liabilities depending on partnership.
3. Governed by Uniformed Partnership Act or Revised Uniformed Partnership Act (RUPA).

Limited Liability Corporation

1. Limited liability
2. Pass through taxation.
3. One or more employees to form an LLC
4. Creation:
    A. File Articles of Organization: See WI Department of Financial Institutions (DFI) online at www.wdfi.org under corporations. Cost $130.00
    B. Operating Agreement: Wisconsin statute 183.0102(16) defines an Operating Agreement as "an agreement in writing, if any, among all of the members as to the conduct of the business of a limited liability company and its relationships with its members." Every LLC should have one.
    C. See the Wisconsin Department of Health Services (DHS) for additional licensing of food safety and recreational licensing at www.dhs.wisconsin.gov. $220.00 for the permit and $400.00 for pre-inspection.

D. Application for WI Business Tax Registration (BTR) $20.00. A Wisconsin tax ID number and a sales permit will be needed. See www.revenue.wi.gov

E. SS-4 Application for Employer Identification Number (EIN) can be found at www.irs.gov

F. To dissolve an LLC use form 510 Articles of Dissolution found at www.wdfi.org. An LLC must dissolve to convert to a corporation.

See the Nolo website http://www.nolo.com/legal-encyclopedia/wisconsin-form-llc-31990.html for guidance on creation of an LLC. Use QuickBooks accounting software for business transactions. An annual report for an LLC is required to be filed with the Department of Financial Institutions.

Corporations

Corporation formation is almost identical to LLC formation using Articles of Incorporation an EIN number, Business Tax Registration and any such needed licenses. The Articles of Incorporation and bylaws are usually written by a promoter and adopted through an act called Novation, which transfers the responsibilities to the directors or shareholders. Corporations are guided by the Model Business Corporation Act (MBCA).

1. Limited liability
2. Double taxation, special pass through taxation as an "S" Corporation.
3. One or more employees to form a Corporation.
4. Creation:
    A. Use a Certificate of Conversion form to convert an LLC to a Chapter "C" corporation. Found at www.dfi.org.
    B. To request Chapter "S" Corporation (special pass through taxation) file form 2553. Found at www.wdfi.org.
    C. To create a Close Corporation see DFI corp59 instructions at www.dfi.org.

D. File a BTR in Wisconsin and EIN with the IRS when starting a new corporation.

E. File DFI Corp form 10 for dissolution of a corporation in Wisconsin.

Writing

Sentences must contain a subject and a verb. Singular nouns take singular verbs. Subject verb object. (Noun verb object.)

Write out the numeral if using o'clock. The meeting begins at eleven o'clock. Use numerals and a.m/p.m if not using o'clock. The meeting begins at 9:30 a.m. Use the numeral if writing exactly on the hour. The meeting will end at 10 a.m.

Use apostrophe to form possessive case of nouns.
Dog's = Owns something; the man's coat (possessive); a child's legal right. For singular nouns that end in "s" form the possessive by adding "s"; the class's performance; Mr. Davis's car.
Dogs = More than one
For plural nouns that end in "s', the classes' performance; the Davises' car.
Dogs' = More than one dog owns it.

Using Id.: Cite case or statute. Refer back to the case or statute by using "Id". To reference a page, use "Id. At 771" or Id. § 912(a). Public Domain uses Paragraph so state Id. at ¶ 69. For example cite the case earlier in the paragraph. Later reference a quote from the case and then state: Id. At 595.-595 being the page number.
Using Hereinafter: Cite case or statute. After the case in parenthesis (hereinafter referred Roc.).
Notes: After case citation in parenthesis: (Holding, quoting, C.J. dissenting, emphasis original, emphasis added).

Active Voice: In the active voice, the subject (noun) of the verb does the action (*They killed the President* & The suspect robbed Bill) (performing the action).
Adjective: A word like *big, red, easy, French,* etc. An adjective describes a noun or pronoun. Adjectives are words that **describe** a noun (i.e. describe person place or thing).
Adverb: A word like *slowly, quietly, well, often,* etc. An adverb modifies a verb. Adverbs are words that describe a verb (i.e. describe an activity).

Auxiliary Verb: A verb that is used with a main verb. *Be, do,* and *have* are auxiliary verbs. *Can, may, must,* etc. are modal auxiliary verbs.

Conjunction: A word used to connect words, phrases and clauses (for example: *and, but, if*).

Modal Verb: An auxiliary verb like *can, may, must,* etc. that modifies the main verb and expresses possibility, probability, etc. It is also called "modal auxiliary verb".

Nouns: Nouns are words that describe a **person, place, or thing**.

Object: In the active voice, a noun or its equivalent that receives the action of the verb. In the passive voice, a noun or its equivalent that does the action of the verb.

Passive Voice: In the passive voice, the subject (noun) receives the action of the verb (*The President was killed & Bill was robbed by the suspect*).*Avoid passive voice.*

Predicate: Each sentence contains (or implies) two parts: a subject and a predicate. The predicate is what is said about the subject.

Preposition: A word like *at, to, in, over,* etc. Prepositions usually come before a noun and give information about things like time, place, and direction.

Pronoun: A word like *I, me, you, he, him, it,* etc. A pronoun replaces a noun.

Pronouns: Word Tense - this refers to a word being past, present, or future tense. I ate, I eat, I will eat.

Subject: Every sentence contains (or implies) two parts: a subject and a predicate. The subject is the main noun (or equivalent) in a sentence about which something is said.

Tense: The form of a verb that shows us when the action or state happens (past, present or future). Note that the name of a tense is not always a guide to when the action happens. The "present continuous tense", for example, can be used to talk about the present or the future.

Verb: A word like *(to) work, (to) love, (to) begin.* A verb describes an action or state. Verbs are **"action" words**.

LEGAL RESEARCH MEMORANDUM

TO: Supervising Attorney

FROM: Name

DATE: March 26, 2012

RE: Analysis of Blue Tooth and Burger Man

               Our File: 11123

QUESTIONS PRESENTED

1. Will Blue Tooth Succeed?
2. Does Burger Man have a case?

CONCLUSIONS

1. Yes. Based on law Blue Tooth will Succeed
2. No. Burger Man was a drunk.

FACTS

Blue Tooth was rightfully minding his own business.

Burger Man was drinking and hit the curb with his car, striking Blue Tooth.

DISCUSSION

Intro to discussion

1. Question presented.

Paragraphs discussing the law.

2. Question presented.

Paragraphs discussing the law.

SUMMARY

Paragraph reiterating memo

NOTE: Anything that may be helpful.

IRAC PARAGRAPH

Broad issue: Will Silly Sam successfully claim he complied with the requirements concerning the return of Tom's security deposit?

Sub-issues/elements:

1. Security deposit withheld.
2. Itemized bill charged with painting and carpeting.
3. Itemized bill postmarked 22 days after Tom moved out.

IRAC PARAGRAPH #1:

Issue: Will Silly Sam successfully prove that he complied with the requirements of the return of Tom's security deposit?

Rule: Wisconsin Statute § 100.20 (5) (2012) allows for twice the amount of pecuniary loss from violation of any administrative rule found under this statute. To comply with a security deposit return under Wis. Admin. Code § ATCP 134.06 (2) (a), (4) (a) (2012), it is required that either a security deposit be returned or a written statement accounting for all withholdings to be mailed within 21 days. Of the statement accounting for all withholding, they must be allowed under the law and not normal wear and tear items found under Wis. Admin. Code § 134.06 (a), (c) (2012).

Application: In this situation, Silly Sam withheld the entire security deposit. Sam's property management company, Tri-County Property Management Company, did send Tom Tepot an itemized bill. This itemized bill has allowable items as described by code and normal wear and tear items that Wisconsin code does not allow. This itemized bill was postmarked 22 days after Tom Tepot moved out.

Conclusion: In order to comply with Wis. Admin. Code § ATCP 134.06 (2) (a), (4) (a) (2012), a landlord must mail out a deposit or detailed notice of withholding a deposit within 21 days. Failure to do so is negligent on behalf of the landowner and may result in pecuniary loss on behalf of the tenant.

IRAC PARAGRAPH #1 PUT TOGETHER

Silly Sam must prove that he complied with the requirements to withhold the return of Tom's security deposit. To comply with the requirements of the return of security deposit, section 134.06 (2) (a) & (4) (a) of the Wisconsin ATCP code requires a return within twenty one days or a written statement accounting for all withholdings. Of the statement accounting for all withholdings, they must be allowed under the law and not normal wear and tear items found under section 134.06 (3) (a) & (c) of the Wisconsin ATCP code. Wisconsin statute § 100.20 (5) allows for twice the amount of pecuniary loss from violation of any administrative rule found under this statute.

In this situation, Silly Sam withheld the entire security deposit. Larry's property management company, Tri-County Property Management Company, did send Tom Teapot an itemized bill. This itemized bill has allowable items as described by code and normal wear and tear items that Wisconsin code does not allow. This itemized bill was postmarked 22 days after Tom Tepot moved out.

Books Used in Class

Legal Research Explained	ISBN 978-0-7355-8767-0
Basic Legal Writing for Paralegals	ISBN 978-0-7355-6738-2
Civil Litigation	ISBN 978-1-111-31222-0
Criminal Law and Procedure	ISBN 978-1-1113127-2-5
Business Organizations for Paralegals	ISBN 978-1-4548-0866-4
Real Estate Law	ISBN 978-1-4390-5720-9

Court Case Abbreviations

CF - Felony - a crime punishable by imprisonment in the Wisconsin state prisons and / or a fine.

CI - Commitment of an Inmate - a case with a petition alleging that a person is a sexually violent person.

CL - Construction Lien - a claim on property for non-payment of work that improved the property.

CM - Misdemeanor - a crime punishable by a fine and-/-or confinement in a local jail, but not by imprisonment in the Wisconsin state prisons.

CO - Condominium Lien - a claim on a condominium unit for the owner's non-payment of assessments for common expenses.

CT - Criminal Traffic - a misdemeanor offense involving the operation of a motor vehicle.

CV - Civil - typically, lawsuits seeking claims in excess of $5,000, but also such actions as restraining orders, appeals from municipal court, and administrative agency decisions, name changes, etc.

CX - Complex Forfeiture - A forfeiture action that requires access to the rules of civil procedure and which is punishable by a forfeiture of money.

FA - Family - divorce, legal separation, annulment, custody, child support, maintenance, property division, or the enforcement or modification of an order affecting the family.

FJ - Foreign Judgment - a judgment or order of a court from a different state, a federal court outside Wisconsin, a municipal court of another county, or a tribal court; treated as if ordered by a Wisconsin circuit court.

FO - Non-Traffic Ordinance Violation - a violation, unrelated to the operation of a motor vehicle, punishable by the forfeiture of money.

GF - Group File - a category for maintaining documents that are not specifically case-related.

HL - Hospital Lien - a claim by a hospital for non-payment of services provided to an injured person. The claim is on a judgment, award, settlement, etc. that the injured person may have against the person responsible for the injury.

HT - Habitual Traffic - No longer available for use. A petition claiming a person is not the person identified by DOT as a habitual traffic offender is now filed as a CV case.

IN - Informal Probate - a typical probate matter in which no issues are contested and a deceased person's estate is administratively handled by the probate registrar instead of by the court.

IP - Incarcerated Person - a case with a petition submitted by a prisoner who wants to begin an action without prepaying court costs and fees.

JD - John Doe - a proceeding under WI Stats. 968.26 To determine whether a crime has been committed. For clerical convenience, this case type also includes the filing of complaints under WI Stats. 968.02(3) and coroners' inquests under WI Stats. 979.04.

JJ - Juvenile Judgment - a judgment against a juvenile for unpaid debt, typically restitution.

JT - Joint Tenancy - No longer available for use. A statement filed with the Register in Probate that results in the termination of a decedent's interest in joint property is filed as a PR case.

ML - Mechanics Lien - No longer available for use. A mechanics lien is not required to be filed with the clerk of circuit court.

OL - Other Lien - claims not specifically identified by the other lien case types and include such claims as environmental liens, mining liens, quarry labor liens, etc.

PA - Paternity - Post judgment actions in paternity cases, such as support and custody. Pre-judgment information concerning the determination of paternity is confidential and is not available to the public.

PR - Probate - formal probate (in which issues are contested and a deceased person's estate is supervised by the court) and such other probate-related actions as the summary settlement of small estates, the termination of joint tenancy, etc.

SC - Small Claims - lawsuits seeking claims of less than $5,000, evictions, and replevin actions (the repossession of property).

TC - Tribal Court Order - a judgment, decision, or order of an Indian tribal court in Wisconsin that is treated as if it had been issued by a Wisconsin state court.

TJ - Transcript of Judgment - a judgment or order from another Wisconsin circuit court, a Wisconsin appellate court, a federal court in Wisconsin, or a municipal court in that county; treated as if ordered by the circuit court in the county where it's filed.

TR - Traffic Forfeiture - a violation, related to the operation of a motor vehicle, punishable by the forfeiture of money.

TW - Tax Warrant - a warrant issued by the Wisconsin Department of Revenue for failure to pay income or franchise tax when due. This warrant has the same effect as a judgment granted by the court.

UC - Unemployment Compensation - a warrant issued by the Wisconsin Department of Workforce Development for an employer's failure to pay contributions, interest, or fees. This warrant has the same effect as a judgment granted by a court.

WC - Workers Compensation - an award issued by the Wisconsin Department of Workforce Development. This award has the same effect as a judgment granted by a court.

WL - Will Filed - a will filed with the court for safekeeping during a person's lifetime.

Definitions

Agent Authority: Actual authority expressly granted by principal (written or oral) or custom.

Agent: agrees to act on principal's behalf, and to be subject to principal's control.

American Rule: Each party covers their own attorney's fees. Statute to reclaim up to $500 in Atty's fees.

Amicus Curie: "Friends of the Court" brief.

Apparent Authority: Really is no authority at all. Only appears to have.

Breach of Contract: Failure, without legal excuse, to perform any promise which forms the whole or part of a contract.

Brief Cases: Facts, History, Issue, Reasoning, Rule.

Case of 1st impression: Court has never decided on a particular issue before.

Case on all fours: 1. Similar facts 2. Similar parties 3. Similar legal issues 4. Similar relief sought. Cook v. Cook

Case on Point: 1. Similar facts 2. Similar legal issues.

Cause remanded: Sending it back to the same court from which it came.

Cashiers check: Check is issued by a bank, the payment of which is guaranteed by the full faith and credit of the bank.

Certified check: Personal check in which the bank certifies the funds are in the account and the check will be honored.

Comparative Negligence: Partial blame. Plaintiff negligence compared to liable party (WI Statute 895).

Concurrence: Agree for different reasons.

Concurrent Sentence: Imprisonment is the length of the longest sentence.

Consecutive Sentence: Imprisonment equals the length of all the sentences.

Conversion: An unauthorized assumption and exercise over the right of ownership over goods or personal items.

Corpus Delicti: A crime must be proven before a person can be convicted of the crime.

DeNovoe: From the beginning.

Dicta: Things that are not part of the holding or reasoning.

Disposition: What court is doing, affirm or reverse, reverse and remand, affirm part, reverse part, modified.

Dissent: Disagree.

Duces Tecum: A court summons ordering the recipient to appear before the court and to bring said documents.

Equitable Remedies: Injunction, specific performance, declaratory relief, etc....

Estoppel: based on failure of principal to take corrective action.

Exculpatory Evidence: Favorable evidence to a criminal defendant.

Express Agreement: Written or oral.

Fiduciary: Duty to act on behalf of and for the benefit of another.

Holding: What court decides (beginning or end of case).

Implied Agreement: Based on behavior.

Inculpatory Evidence: Unfavorable evidence to a criminal defendant.

In Forma Pauperis: Someone who is without the funds to pursue the normal costs of a lawsuit or a criminal defense. Also known as Indigency in which counsel will be provided if it cannot be afforded.

Injunction: Order for defendant to do or refrain from doing an act.

Injunction: Court orders someone to stop doing the act.

In Rem: Jurisdiction over property.

Majority: Judicial opinion of over half the members of the court.

Percuriam (Per Curiam Decision): Written by the court (appeals) rather than by the judge.

Precedent: Previously decided cases.

Plurality: More than any other group.

Precedent: previously decided case.

Preemption/pre-emption: Federal law controls over state law.

Principal: The person on whose behalf the agent acts.

Ratified Authority: Granted by principal after the fact.

Reasoning: Ratio Decendi.

Rescission: Contract canceled damages.

Specific Performance: Order to perform what was promised;-it is unique and used when money is not adequate. Can be used for a person withholding property and ordered to return it.

Stare Decisis: Let the decision stand (precedence). Should follow precedent unless good reason not to.

Sureties: Agree to pay someone else's debt.

Unjust enrichment Doctrine: One person should not enrich themselves at the expense of others and should make restitution for property or benefits received.

Vicarious liability: Strict secondary liability, superior responsible for acts of subordinate.

Writ of Certiorari: Granting cert or review of the court.

Unlawful Detainer: Action brought by landlord to evict a tenant.

www.ingramcontent.com/pod-product-compliance
Lightning Source LLC
Chambersburg PA
CBHW060159290526
45789CB00003B/1088